# Rain or Shine!

## by Jan Bloom

Welcome to the Lab! To start using your Weather Station right away, turn to page 22!

...orthup Way, Bellevue, Washington. Published 2005.

...ab®, an imprint of becker&mayer!
...erved. SmartLab® is a registered trademark of becker&mayer!, 11010 Northup Way, Bellevue, Washington.
...tive development by Jim Becker and Anna Johnson

If you have questions or comments about this product, send e-mail to info@smartlabtoys.com or visit www.smartlabtoys.com.

Edited by Ben Grossblatt
Written by Jan Bloom
Art direction and packaging design by Scott Westgard
Designed and illustrated by Eddee Helms
Assembly illustrations by John Laidlaw
Product photography by Keith Megay
SmartLab® character photography by Craig Harrold
Product development by Mark Byrnes
Production management by Katie Stephens
Project management by Beth Lenz
Design assistance by Karrie Lee

Image credits: Page 14: Tornado background courtesy of the National Oceanic and Atmospheric Administration (NOAA)/Department of Commerce. Page 15: Hurricane background courtesy of NOAA/Department of Commerce; Hurricane satellite image courtesy of NASA. Page 19: Ozone layer courtesy of NASA. Page 21: Weather satellite and Doppler radar images courtesy of NOAA/Department of Commerce.

Every effort has been made to correctly attribute all the material reproduced in this book. We will be happy to correct any errors in future editions.

Printed, manufactured, and assembled in China.

Rain or Shine! is part of the SmartLab® Weather Station kit. Not to be sold separately.

10 9 8 7 6 5 4 3
1-932855-25-4
05260

# WHAT IS WEATHER?

Weather is what's happening in the Earth's atmosphere at one place and time. It seems like everyone talks about the weather, but most people don't know much about it. With the help of your Weather Station and this book, you'll learn a lot about how weather happens and have fun doing it. When you're done, you'll be able to track the wind, chart temperature changes, and measure rainfall.

Rain or snow, fog or sunshine, no matter where you live, the weather affects you every day. That's why the study of weather is so important.

**The Earth is** inside an envelope of air called the *atmosphere* (AT-muss-fear). Changes in the atmosphere create weather. Even though the Sun is millions of miles away, it's the most important element of weather and it affects our atmosphere. *Solar* energy (energy from the Sun) makes clouds form and winds blow.

Imagine you're standing at the bottom of a lake. (Also imagine you're wearing scuba equipment, so you can breathe down there.) All around, you can feel the currents of water moving through the lake. The Earth's atmosphere is like the water in the lake. But instead of water, it's made up of gases that help maintain life on Earth. The movement and flow of these gases creates the weather.

# THE WIND

## WIND IS AIR IN MOTION

Wind is the way air gets from one place to another. When the Sun heats the air, it expands and rises like a balloon. As the heated air rises, colder air rushes in and takes its place. Then, the warm air cools down and falls back toward the Earth. This cycle of heating and cooling, rising and falling, is called *convection*. Convection creates large masses of moving air, or wind.

## AIR PRESSURE

Air that's close to the Earth has the weight of all the air above it pressing it down. This force is called *air pressure*. The higher up you go in the atmosphere, the less air pressure there is because there's less air above it pushing it down.

Airplanes fly high where the air is thin. To help airplane passengers breathe easily, airplanes have pressurized air.

### ❖ WEATHER LORE ❖

*Wind before rain, fair weather again.*

Whenever there's a strong wind before it rains, it shows that the rain clouds are being moved along by the wind so the storm should pass quickly.

4

# HIGHS AND LOWS

A large area or mass of high-pressure air is called a *high*. High-pressure areas are made of air that is cooling and sinking. Highs usually bring clear weather. Low-pressure masses, called *lows*, are made of warming air that is rising. They usually bring stormy weather.

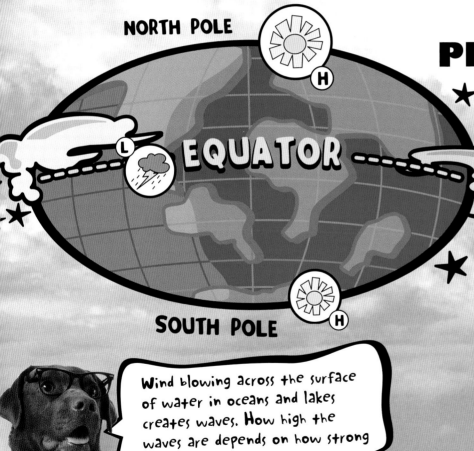

NORTH POLE

EQUATOR

SOUTH POLE

Wind blowing across the surface of water in oceans and lakes creates waves. How high the waves are depends on how strong the wind is blowing.

# PRESSURE AND WINDFLOW

Pressure differences in the atmosphere make the wind move or flow. When atmospheric pressure is high, the air is squashed together. This squashed, high-pressure air flows toward places where the pressure is lower. As air flows from one area to another, the pressure gradually changes. As one area gets warmer, another cools down. There are always changing patterns of high and low air pressure moving around the Earth.

However, within this pattern, there are some things that don't change. At the equator, an imaginary line around the Earth halfway between the North and South Poles, there is a constant band of low pressure. At the poles, there is permanent high pressure.

# TEMPERATURE

## ENERGY FROM THE SUN CREATES
## TEMPERATURE

Think of the Sun as a gigantic furnace that pumps heat and light in all directions. Less than a billionth of the Sun's heat and light energy actually reaches the Earth. A lot of the Sun's energy that does reach the Earth bounces back into space. Most of what doesn't bounce back is absorbed by the atmosphere and heats the air. You can feel the Sun's energy as it warms your skin when you sit in a sunny window.

**WEATHER RECORD**

THE HIGHEST temperature ever recorded on Earth was 136°F (58°C), at Al Aziziyah, Libya, in 1922.

# WATER—
## A KEY WEATHER INGREDIENT

*Precipitation* (pre-sip-uh-TAY-shin) is water that falls from the sky. Rain, snow, sleet, and hail are different forms of precipitation *and* different forms of water.

Parts of the hottest months of the year are called **dog days**.

The fact that water can take many forms is one of the things that make weather, well, weather. Water can be a solid (ice), a liquid (water) and a gas (water vapor). Water falls to Earth, where it is heated by the Sun and changed into water vapor. The water vapor returns to the atmosphere and forms new clouds.

# FAHRENHEIT
## AND CELSIUS

Thermometers are **instruments** used to measure temperature, or the degree of hotness or coldness of an object. About 300 years ago, Gabriel Fahrenheit used mercury to make the first thermometer. He marked a scale and used his thermometer to measure different forms of water. On his Fahrenheit (F) scale, salt water freezes at 0°F and pure water freezes at 32°F and boils at 212°F.

Panting helps dogs cool off. Because dogs don't sweat, they get rid of excess heat in their bodies by panting. The heat turns the water in their mouths into water vapor and it evaporates.

**Anders Celsius created** the Celsius or Centigrade (C) temperature scale a few years later. In his system of measurement, pure water freezes at 0°C and boils at 100°C.

**The United States** is one of the few countries that still use the Fahrenheit scale.

**WEATHER RECORD**

**THE COLDEST** temperature on Earth was measured in the Antarctic. It was -129°F (-89.4°C).

## CONVERTING FROM FAHRENHEIT TO CELSIUS

**Here's how to change a Fahrenheit temperature to Celsius.**

**Step 1:** Subtract 32 from the Fahrenheit temperature.

**Step 2:** Multiply the difference by $5/9$ (which is about .56).

**EXAMPLE:** **What is 80°F in Celsius?**
- 80 – 32 = 48
- 48 x .56 = 26.88
- 80°F is about 27°C

# RAIN

Raindrops form in clouds, one tiny droplet at a time. They begin to take shape when the water vapor in the cloud sticks to a speck of dust, smoke, or salt. Inside the cloud, the heaviest droplets fall slowly. Then air inside the cloud pushes the droplets up again. More and more water droplets join together to get bigger and heavier. Eventually, the droplets become heavy enough to fall from the cloud.

## RAINBOWS—
### LIGHT, WATER, AND AIR

Sometimes when light and water meet in the sky you can see a curved band of colored light called a rainbow. Rainbows usually happen during or right after a rain shower when the sun is shining and there is water in the air. Even though sunlight looks like it is clear or white, it is actually made of the complete spectrum of color. Sunlight includes red, orange, yellow, green, blue, indigo, and violet. When the sunlight bounces off the droplets of water, it separates the light into the color spectrum, and you see a rainbow.

### WEATHER LORE

***Rainbow in the morning, Sailor's warning.***
***Rainbow at night, Sailor's delight.***

When sunlight creates a rainbow it bounces off of water droplets. In the morning, rainbows are in the west because the Sun rises in the eastern sky. In the evening, rainbows are in the east because it's the setting Sun in the west that creates the rainbow. Even though rain can come from any direction, most storms move from west to east. So a sailor, or anyone who sees a rainbow in the morning, can expect it to rain. When the setting Sun creates a rainbow to the east, the clouds have already passed so it won't rain.

# ACID RAIN

Factories, homes, cars, trucks, and buses burn fuels that send some poisonous gases into the air. These poisons combine with water in the atmosphere and become part of rain, snow, or fog. Then, when the poisoned water, called *acid rain*, falls to the ground it damages the environment. Acid rain can destroy the leaves of plants, kill trees, pollute the soil, and change the chemistry of lakes and streams. When that happens, animals, fish, and other wildlife die. Acid rain can also damage buildings and statues.

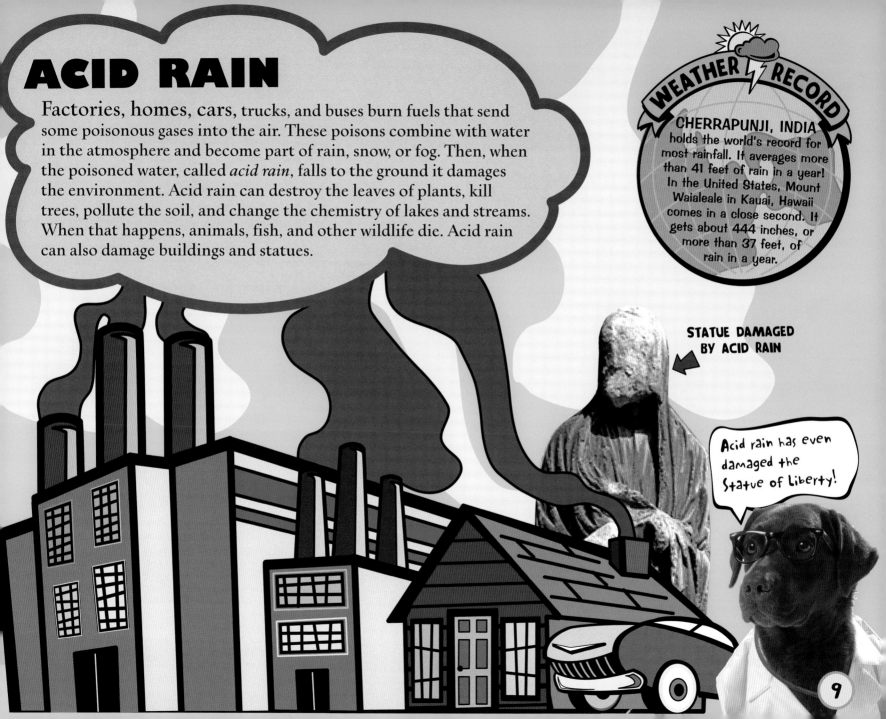

## WEATHER RECORD

CHERRAPUNJI, INDIA holds the world's record for most rainfall. It averages more than 41 feet of rain in a year! In the United States, Mount Waialeale in Kauai, Hawaii comes in a close second. It gets about 444 inches, or more than 37 feet, of rain in a year.

STATUE DAMAGED BY ACID RAIN

Acid rain has even damaged the Statue of Liberty!

# SNOW AND ICE

## SNOW—

### FROZEN WATER CRYSTALS

Snowflakes are made of tiny crystals of frozen water vapor that form around bits of dirt or dust, like raindrops do. Almost every raindrop begins as a snowflake because the temperature is very cold up where most clouds form. Snow crystals grow until they're heavy enough to begin their trip to the ground. Snowflakes come in many shapes but every one is different!

When snowflakes form in air that is below freezing all the way from the cloud to the ground, they fall slowly and build up, or accumulate, on the ground. But if the air near the ground is warmer, the snowflakes melt on the way down and become softer, wetter snowflakes, sleet, or freezing rain.

WATER VAPOR

DIRT PARTICLE

IF THE SNOWFLAKE HITS COLD AIR ON THE WAY DOWN . . .

IF THE SNOWFLAKE HITS WARMER AIR ON THE WAY DOWN . . .

. . . YOU GET SNOW.

. . . YOU GET FREEZING RAIN.

No two snowflakes are identical because every snowflake takes its own path from the clouds to the Earth.

Can you tell the difference?

## ❄ WEATHER LORE ❄

*Pale moon rains, Red moon blows.*
*White moon neither rains or snows.*

On a night when the air is dirtier or dustier, the moon looks pale or reddish, When the air is clean, the moon looks white. The dustier the air, the greater the chance that precipitation will form.

# SLEET AND FREEZING RAIN

If partially melted snowflakes or raindrops fall through a layer of air near the ground that is colder, they can freeze again and turn to sleet. Sleet is clear pellets of ice.

It can snow in Florida! On January 19, 1977, West Palm Beach, Florida had its first snowfall ever. At Miami's Crandon Park Zoo they used special heat lamps to keep the iguanas warm!

Sometimes the colder layer of air near the ground is shallow. When that happens, there isn't enough time for the melting snowflakes or raindrops to freeze into sleet. Instead, they hit the ground as freezing rain. Freezing rain is very dangerous. When it hits the cold ground, it spreads out and becomes a thin film of slippery ice that can cause automobile accidents.

WEATHER RECORD

THOMPSON PASS, ALASKA got almost 187 inches of snow (more than 15 feet!) in one week of February 1953.

# STORMS

## THUNDERSTORMS

Thunderstorms are powerful electrical storms designed by nature to create balance in the atmosphere. They pump warm, moist air from the lower atmosphere into the upper atmosphere and they bring cold, dry air from the upper atmosphere down to the lower atmosphere.

COLD, DRY AIR
PUMPED DOWN

WARM, MOIST AIR
IS PUMPED UP

## LIGHTNING

POSITIVE CHARGE

POSITIVE CHARGE

NEGATIVE CHARGE    ELECTRICAL CURRENT

On hot days, when the ground heats up quickly, bubbles of hot air float up and create convection currents. As air molecules crash into each other, negatively charged electrons are knocked off and they collect in the bottoms of clouds. Lightning, an intense electrical current, travels from the negatively charged cloud to the positively charged ground. Lightning is hotter than the surface of the sun, and the superheated air around it expands so fast it explodes. We call that explosion thunder.

During a lightning storm, the safest place for you to be is inside!

# HAIL

Unlike sleet, which can only form in cold winter weather, hail occurs in spring, summer, and fall. Hailstones are created by the convection in huge thunderclouds that reach up into the atmosphere where the temperature is below freezing. Each hailstone is actually a raindrop that's been frozen over and over again by bouncing up and down in thunderclouds. As the drops bounce up and down, they are coated again and again by more raindrops that freeze as the wind pushes them back up into the cloud.

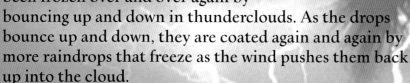

If you sliced open a hailstone, you'd find rings of ice inside. The number of rings tells you how many up-and-down trips the hailstone made in the thundercloud.

## HOW FAR AWAY IS IT?

You can estimate how far away lightning strikes are by counting from one to five. As soon as you see a flash of lightning, start counting. Count one number for each second. If you can count to five before you hear thunder, the lightning strike is about a mile away. If you can count to ten, it's about two miles. If you only get to two or three, the lightning struck close by!

## ❊ WEATHER LORE ❊

*When clouds appear like rocks and towers,*
*The earth will be washed by frequent showers.*

On your cloud chart, find the Cumulonimbus (KYOOM-yoo-lo-NIM-bus) cloud. These are the mountainous clouds described by this saying. They often bring big thunderstorms.

# EXTREME AND

Most days, the weather is unexciting. But weather can also pack a real punch. Extreme weather such as tornadoes, hurricanes, or monsoons can do a lot of damage.

## TORNADOES

Tornadoes can happen when the energy inside a cloud creates an updraft—a sucking-in-and-up of air. All the air pulled up into the cloud spins and twists. All that twisting air is a tornado. Winds inside a tornado can spin at more than 300 mph. Most tornadoes strike in an area of the United States called Tornado Alley. It includes parts of South Dakota, Minnesota, Wyoming, Nebraska, Iowa, Colorado, Oklahoma, New Mexico, and Texas.

> T. Theodore Fujita developed a scale for classifying the strength of tornadoes.

### FUJITA TORNADO SCALE

| SCALE | WIND SPEED | DAMAGE |
|---|---|---|
| F0-Gale Tornado | 40-72mph | Chimneys damaged, branches break off trees, some trees blow over |
| F1-Moderate Tornado | 73-112mph | Wind peels surface off roofs, moving autos pushed off roads, attached garages may be destroyed |
| F2-Significant Tornado | 113-157mph | Roofs torn off frame houses, freight cars pushed over, large trees snapped or uprooted |
| F3-Severe Tornado | 158-206mph | Roofs and some walls torn off well-constructed houses, trains overturned, most trees in forest uprooted |
| F4-Devastating Tornado | 207-260mph | Well-constructed houses leveled, cars thrown |
| F5-Incredible Tornado | 261-318mph | Strong-frame houses lifted off foundations and carried considerable distances, concrete structures badly damaged |

# WILD WEATHER

## MONSOONS CHANGE DIRECTION

A monsoon is a type of wind that reverses direction seasonally. The best example of a monsoon occurs in the Indian Ocean and southern Asia. In warm summer months, a moist southwest wind blows from the ocean toward the land and brings heavy rain. Sometimes it rains so much that it causes floods that affect billions of people. In the winter, the dry monsoon wind blows from the land toward the ocean.

**HURRICANE**

## HURRICANES

Hurricanes start over warm ocean water when a group of big thunderstorms comes together and the wind picks up speed. Once the winds reach 74 mph, what was called a tropical storm becomes an official hurricane. In the last ten years, improvements in technology have helped meteorologists predict the path a hurricane will take. But because hurricane winds can get very strong, they sometimes go off in another direction.

Since 1979, hurricanes have been called by both men's and women's names. They are always named in alphabetical order. (But **Q**, **U**, and **Z** aren't used.) If a hurricane does a lot of damage, its name is never given to another hurricane. Fabian, Isabel, and Juan are hurricane names that were retired in 2003.

A hurricane watch means there could be a hurricane in the next 36 hours. During a hurricane warning, a hurricane is expected within 24 hours and people in its path may be told to leave the area.

# WEATHER AROUND

Different parts of the world have different climates. That means they have different weather.

## CLIMATE

Some parts of the world have deserts. Others have rainforests. Did you ever wonder why? The reason is *climate* (KLY-mitt). Climate is the weather a place has over a long period of time. It includes the general pattern of weather in the area, its seasons, and extremes like droughts or rainy periods. An area's climate has a lot to do with the atmosphere near the Earth's surface.

## HOT OR COLD

The amount of sunlight that reaches a place helps determine its climate. The equator has a temperature that is almost always the same because the Sun's rays hit it directly. In places where the Sun's rays hit the Earth at an angle, the warmth of the Sun isn't as strong. The closer you move to the North or South Pole (that is, the farther you go from the equator), the colder it is.

| |
|---|
| Deserts get less than 10 inches of rain in a year. |
| Deserts are hot in the day and cold at night. |
| The Saguaro Cactus only grows in the Sonoran Desert in North America. It can live to be 200 years old but it only blooms once. |

The Sahara Desert is the largest desert in the world. It's located in North Africa and covers about 3,250,000 square miles. (It's almost as big as the whole United States!)

# THE WORLD

## WET OR DRY

An area's climate also depends on how much precipitation it gets. In addition to heat from the Sun, the Earth's climate system is created by atmospheric circulation—wind—that moves hot and cold air masses around the globe. Wet areas, like rainforests and jungles, are located in places where these traveling masses of air meet and create rain clouds.

## CLIMATE ZONES

Climates are grouped into zones that share similar features.

There is always ice in the *polar* zone and only a short time in the summer when the temperature rises above freezing. Parts of northern Canada and Siberia are in the polar zone.

People who like warm weather visit the *tropical* zone where the temperature doesn't change much from season to season. The southwestern United States, islands in the Caribbean Sea, southern Africa, and northern Australia are in the tropical zone.

Places in the *temperate* zone have four very different seasons with hot summers and cold, snowy winters. Much of Western Europe and the United States is in the temperate zone

Sahara Desert

WEATHER RECORD

**THE EAST ANTARCTIC ICE SHEET** is the single, largest sheet of ice on Earth. In some places, it's almost three miles thick!

# GLOBAL

## WHAT'S A GREENHOUSE?

Plants that wouldn't be able to survive outside can grow in a greenhouse—a building with a roof and sides made from glass. Greenhouses work by trapping heat from the Sun, like a car that's parked in sunlight. The glass allows the heat energy and light from the Sun to enter the greenhouse but prevents it from escaping, so the plants stay warm enough to live through the winter.

## THE GREENHOUSE EFFECT

A shifting balance of energy between the planet and our atmosphere creates the climate. The Sun heats the Earth's surface and the Earth radiates that heat back into space. Like the glass in the greenhouse, gases in the atmosphere trap some heat.

Over centuries, there have been cycles of extreme heat and cold. When they occur, life on Earth changes dramatically. Just 18,000 years ago, parts of Europe and the North American continent were covered with ice. So much water was stored in these *glaciers* (GLAY-shurs), that the sea level was about 400 feet lower!

18

# WARMING

## GREENHOUSE GASES

Recently, the amount of carbon dioxide, methane, and nitrous oxide—the "greenhouse" gases that trap heat in the atmosphere—has increased. Having more greenhouse gases in the atmosphere has made the Earth hotter. That's because there are more gases to trap heat in the atmosphere.

Many scientists believe human activity has created the increase in greenhouse gases. We burn coal, oil, and gas to heat buildings, run cars, and power factories. Burning these fuels releases greenhouse gases into the atmosphere.

If the Earth's temperature gets a lot hotter, the glaciers could melt. Water from the glaciers could cause the ocean to rise. The melting glaciers could eventually flood the planet.

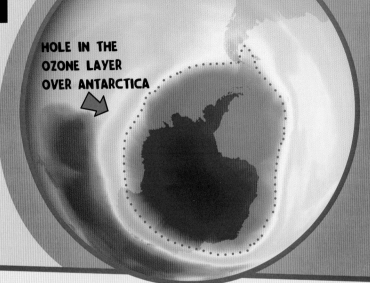

HOLE IN THE OZONE LAYER OVER ANTARCTICA

Ozone is a gas in our atmosphere that protects humans and other living things on our planet by absorbing harmful ultraviolet light from the Sun. Scientists believe the amount of ozone in our atmosphere is shrinking because chemicals we have released into the air destroy it.

## THINGS YOU CAN DO TO SLOW
## GLOBAL WARMING

MOST OF US CAN DO SOMETHING TO REDUCE THE AMOUNT OF GREENHOUSE GAS WE PUT INTO THE ATMOSPHERE.

➤ WHEN YOU CAN, WALK, USE YOUR BICYCLE, RIDE IN A CARPOOL, OR TAKE THE BUS.

➤ TURN OFF LIGHTS, THE TELEVISION, AND THE COMPUTER WHEN YOU FINISH USING THEM.

➤ PLANT MORE TREES—THEY ABSORB CARBON DIOXIDE FROM THE AIR.

➤ RECYCLE CANS, PLASTIC BOTTLES AND BAGS, NEWSPA-PERS, CARDBOARD, GLASS, AND METAL.

➤ LEARN MORE ABOUT RENEWABLE ENERGY RESOURCES LIKE WIND, SOLAR, AND WAVE POWER.

➤ ENCOURAGE THE PEOPLE YOU KNOW TO BUY PRODUCTS THAT ARE SPECIALLY MADE TO SAVE ENERGY.

# METEOROLOGY

**Day and night,** for thousands of years, people have watched the sky and tracked the weather.

## METEOROLOGY

The study of weather is called *meteorology* (MEET-ee-or-OL-uh-jee). Scientists who examine the weather and predict how it will change are called *meteorologists*. They use special instruments to collect information from different parts of the atmosphere. Meteorologists also learn about the weather history of a place. Knowing what happened in the past helps them identify patterns and predict what might happen in the future.

> Weather stations launch weather ballons every day. These special balloons tell meteorologists about temperature, humidity, and wind speed.

**WEATHER RECORD**

A CARTOON CHARACTER named Woolly Lamb gave the very first TV weather forecast in the United States.

# DOPPLER RADAR, SATELLITES, AND COMPUTERS

Meteorologists use Doppler radar, weather satellites, and computers to tell them what's happening on and around Earth. Satellites orbit the Earth and take pictures of the atmosphere. Doppler radar bounces signals off of rain, snow, bugs, and anything else in the air to create another kind of picture of the location and strength of growing storms. All of this information is put into computers that draw models meteorologists use to predict the weather.

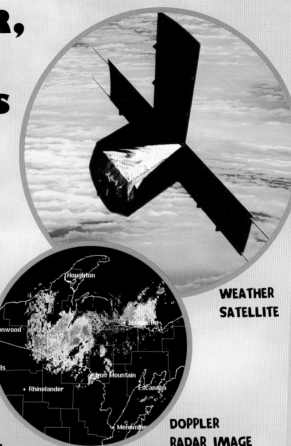

WEATHER SATELLITE

DOPPLER RADAR IMAGE

## ALL WEATHER, ALL THE TIME

Now you know that weather never stops. Maybe that's one reason people are always interested in it. Today there are places you can go to find out what weather events are happening anywhere in the world. There are television channels, radio stations, and web sites that give you weather information 24 hours a day.

**NOW IT'S TIME TO PUT YOUR WEATHER STATION TOGETHER AND LEARN HOW TO USE IT!**

**CAN ANYONE MAKE IT RAIN?**
There was once a man called the rainmaker. Charles Mallory Hatfield earned his title in 1904 when he promised the people of Los Angeles that he could end their drought within four months. Hatfield built a tower and sent his secret mixture of chemicals into the sky. It started to rain almost immediately! Other people hired him and he traveled all over. Hatfield said he was responsible for more than 500 successful rainmaking events. Today, meteorologists don't believe that Hatfield had a secret formula to make it rain. They think he was just a very lucky man.

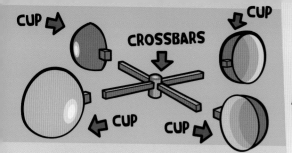

CUP
CUP
CROSSBARS
CUP
CUP

# ASSEMBLY
## INSTRUCTIONS

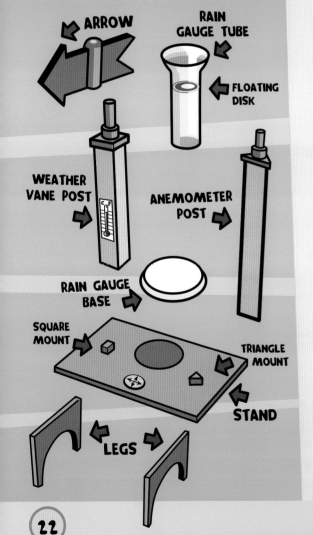

ARROW

RAIN GAUGE TUBE

FLOATING DISK

WEATHER VANE POST

ANEMOMETER POST

RAIN GAUGE BASE

SQUARE MOUNT

TRIANGLE MOUNT

STAND

LEGS

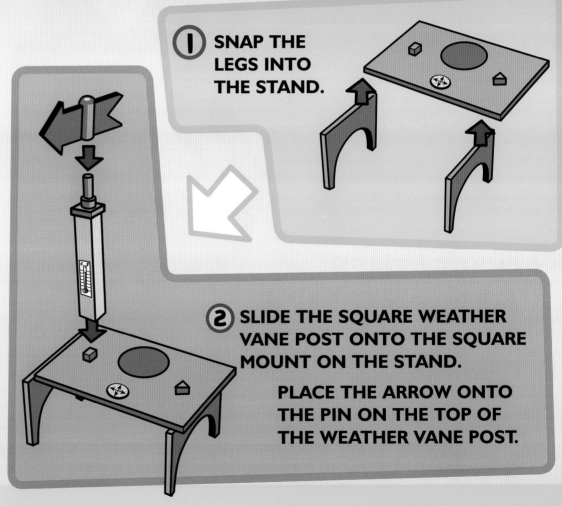

① SNAP THE LEGS INTO THE STAND.

② SLIDE THE SQUARE WEATHER VANE POST ONTO THE SQUARE MOUNT ON THE STAND.

PLACE THE ARROW ONTO THE PIN ON THE TOP OF THE WEATHER VANE POST.

**3** SLIDE THE TRIANGLE ANEMOMETER POST ONTO THE TRIANGLE MOUNT ON THE STAND.

**4** ASSEMBLE THE ANENOMETER BY SNAPPING THE CUPS ONTO THE ENDS OF THE CROSSBARS.

MAKE SURE ALL THE CUPS FACE THE SAME DIRECTION. SLIDE THE CROSSBARS WITH CUPS ATTACHED ONTO THE PIN ON THE TOP OF THE ANEMOMETER POST

**5** ASSEMBLE THE RAIN GAUGE BY SNAPPING THE TUBE ONTO THE FLAT BASE.

SET THE RAIN GAUGE WITH THE BASE IN ITS PLACE ON TOP OF THE STAND.

**FINISHED!**

# USING YOUR

## WIND DIRECTION

When the wind blows, it pushes against the weather vane on your weather station. This makes the arrow swivel and point in the direction the wind is blowing.

Compare the weather vane arrow to the directions on the compass. This tells you what direction the wind is blowing. (Unlike your Weather Station, when weather reports give wind directions, they're talking about the direction the wind is blowing *from*.)

## WIND SPEED

The anemometer (an-uh-MOM-uh-ter) on your Weather Station measures how fast the wind is blowing. Wind blows into the cups and spins the arms around. The harder the wind blows, the faster the anemometer spins.

**USE THIS TABLE TO FIND OUT HOW FAST THE WIND IS BLOWING.**

| IF: | THEN THE WIND IS BLOWING THIS FAST |
|---|---|
| You can follow the one orange cup with your eyes as the anemometer spins . . . | Between 0 and 5 miles per hour |
| You can't follow the one orange cup with your eyes, but the cups aren't spinning fast enough to blur together . . . | Between 5 and 10 miles per hour |
| The cups blur together into one donut-shaped disk as the anemometer spins . . . | Over 10 miles per hour |

# WEATHER STATION

## TEMPERATURE

To find the temperature using your Weather Station, look at the thermometer mounted on the weather vane post. Find the number next to the top of the line of colored liquid. That number is the temperature and it is marked in both Fahrenheit and Celsius.

## RAIN

Your Weather Station's rain gauge can show you quickly and clearly how much rain has fallen. The little floating disk inside shows you the amount of rainfall. The gauge is marked. Find the mark next to the floating disk. That's how much rain has fallen. Empty your rain gauge often. It holds half an inch of rain when it's full.

An average raindrop contains way more than 10 million cloud droplets.

# WEATHER WORDS

## HUMIDITY

Have you ever heard anyone say, "It's not the heat, it's the humidity that's making me feel so hot"? *Humidity* (hyoo-MID-uh-tee) is the word meteorologists use to describe the amount of water vapor in the air. When the humidity is low, there is less water vapor in the air so the sweat on your body is able to evaporate quickly. When the humidity is high, it takes longer for your sweat to evaporate, so you feel hotter (and sticky).

## FRONTS

Weather events, like rain and snow, usually happen when a mass of warm air (a low) meets a mass of cold air (a high). The place these two air masses meet is called a *front*. When they meet, the two different air masses struggle for control at the front.

Cold fronts are created when the cold air mass cools down the warm air it meets. The cold air pushes the warm air upwards. When that happens, the warm air cools down quickly and forms clouds that give off short bursts of heavy precipitation.

Warm fronts are created when the warm air pushes itself up over the cold air. As it rises, the warm air cools down slowly. This often creates steady, widespread precipitation that can last for several hours.

# WEATHER SYMBOLS

Have you noticed that weather maps have funny-looking lines or symbols on them? Each one of them represents a weather condition like snow or rain. These symbols tell you what the weather in different places is like.

**BELOW ARE THE MOST COMMON SYMBOLS METEOROLOGISTS USE.**

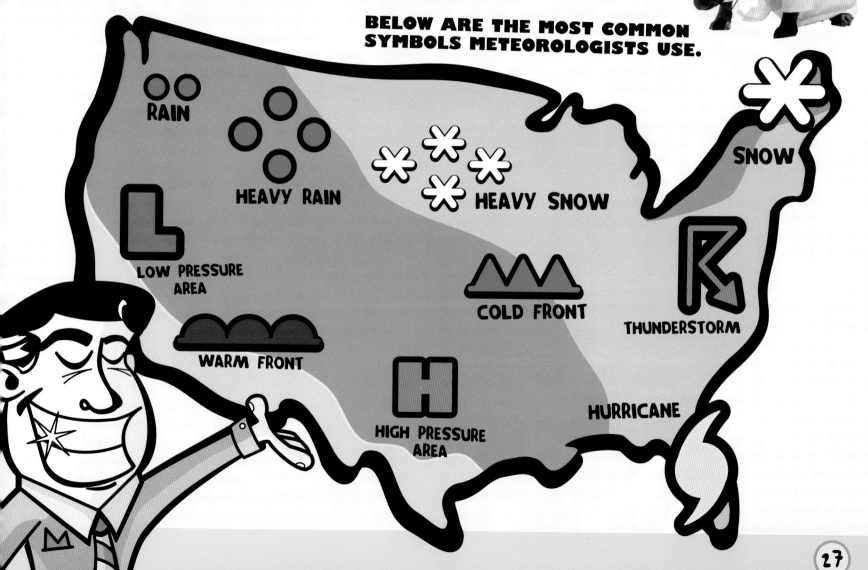

RAIN

HEAVY RAIN

HEAVY SNOW

SNOW

LOW PRESSURE AREA

COLD FRONT

THUNDERSTORM

WARM FRONT

HIGH PRESSURE AREA

HURRICANE

# WEATHER PROJECTS

With your Weather Station, you can check the temperature, track the wind, find out how much rain fell on your home, and identify weather patterns. Here are some ideas to get you started.

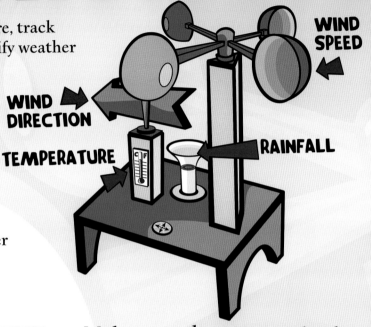

WIND SPEED

WIND DIRECTION

TEMPERATURE

RAINFALL

## PROJECT 1
# CHART THE WEATHER!

Keep track of the readings you take with your Weather Station by making your own weather observation chart and using it to find patterns in your local weather. Begin by making a grid that looks like this:

## WEATHER OBSERVATION CHART

| DATE | TIME | TEMPERATURE | WIND SPEED | WIND DIRECTION | RAINFALL | CLOUD TYPE |
|------|------|-------------|------------|----------------|----------|------------|
|      |      |             |            |                |          |            |
|      |      |             |            |                |          |            |
|      |      |             |            |                |          |            |
|      |      |             |            |                |          |            |
|      |      |             |            |                |          |            |
|      |      |             |            |                |          |            |

Make your chart big enough to last one month. Set your Weather Station up in the same place each time you use it. Take your reading of wind speed and wind direction, temperature, and rainfall at the same time each day. After the month is over, you'll have a set of weather data that you can work with. Can you find any patterns in the data? Did it rain more when it was warmer or cooler? Is there a connection between the temperature and wind speed?

# PROJECT 2
# WIND DIRECTION
## AND THE WEATHER

Using the data you recorded in your Weather Chart, see if you can answer this question:

### Can you see any connection between the wind's direction and the weather?

Never take readings or measurements from your Weather Station during stormy weather. Stay inside when the weather's bad.

Make a new page in your weather observation chart that gives you two or three places to record wind direction each day. See if you can observe and record wind direction three times every day for the next week. For example, you could check the wind direction after breakfast, when you come home from school, and before you have dinner. Once you have data for a week, compare the wind direction with the weather you've recorded. What happened to the weather when the wind changed direction?

# MAKE A WEATHER MAP

Watch the weather report on television or look it up in the newspaper.
Then use the symbols you learned and draw your own weather map.

## PROJECT 4
# BEAT THE WEATHERMAN

Find out if the meteorologists on the local news or in the paper are right. Keep track of their predictions and see how they match up with the readings you take with your Weather Station. Can you use your data to predict tomorrow's weather? See if you agree with the meteorologists. Who's right more often?

## PROJECT 5
# SIX-LEGGED THERMOMETERS

Did you know that crickets can be accurate thermometers? But you have to know the code to figure out the temperature. First, you count how many times a cricket chirps in 15 seconds. Then, add 37. Whatever number you get for a total is the temperature in degrees Fahrenheit. And it's completely accurate! Or, maybe not *completely* accurate. Some people say to add 37; others say to add 40. Still others say to add 48. To check it, observe crickets in your area and see if you can figure out the correct formula.

# DO-IT-YOURSELF
## WEATHER REPORTS

Okay! You've learned about wind and water in our atmosphere. You've seen the forms weather can take around the globe. You've conducted weather experiments. Now it's time to let the world know what you've found. That's right—it's time to make your own weather reports!

> They say everyone talks about the weather, but no one ever does anything about it. Well, not anymore!

## THE
# WEATHER TRACKER

Use your weather tracker to notify everyone— or, well, everyone in your house—of current weather conditions.

## WEATHER STICKERS

Make a weather journal and use these stickers to keep track of each day's main weather.

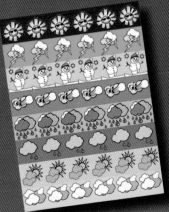

## CLOUD CHART

This chart will help you identify the clouds you spot!

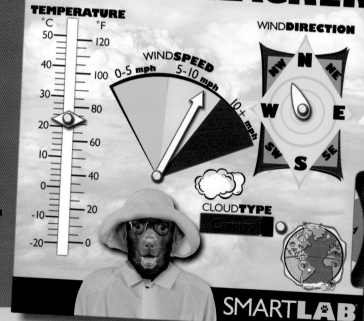